The Nature Kid's Guide to
HAWKS

DAVID ANDERSON

LP Media Inc. Publishing
Text copyright © 2026 by LP Media Inc.

For information address LP Media Inc. Publishing,
30012 Variolite St NW, Princeton MN 55371
www.lpmedia.org

Publication Data

Hawks
The Nature Kid's Guide to Hawks — First edition.

Summary: "Learn all about Hawks, the Nature Kid Way"
— Provided by publisher.

ISBN: 979-8-89818-208-3

[1. Hawks – Non-Fiction] I. Title.

Title: The Nature Kid's Guide to Hawks

CONTENTS

SKY STALKERS

Hawks can spot a rabbit from over a mile away — that's like seeing a penny from 20 football fields!

Scree! A hawk glides high over the treetops on wide wings.

Hawks are **raptors**, which means they hunt other animals for food. These strong birds live all over the world, from hot deserts to cold mountains. The south pole is the only place in the world that has none.

Hawks come in many sizes. Some are small, while others spread their wings as wide as a door. Most have brown or gray feathers that help them blend into trees and rocks.

Look up on your next walk. You might see a hawk sitting on a pole or fence. It is watching the ground, waiting for its next meal to move!

RAPTOR REVEALED

A hawk's feathers weigh more than all of its bones put together!

Swoosh! A hawk flaps its wings and soars above the ground.

A hawk's body is built for flying. Their bones are hollow and light. This helps them stay up in the air without working too hard.

Feathers do many jobs for a hawk. Soft down feathers keep a hawk warm. Long wing feathers help it glide and turn fast. Tail feathers work like a rudder, helping the hawk steer left and right.

Hawks have strong chest muscles too. These muscles power each wing beat. That is how a hawk can fly fast, make quick turns, and chase down **prey**.

BUILT TO HUNT

Snap! A hawk spots a mouse and gets ready to swoop down and attack.

Hawks have tools made for hunting. Their sharp, curved **talons** grip prey tight. A hooked beak rips food into small bites. Together, these tools help them catch and eat a meal in minutes.

A hawk's eyes are its best tool. They can see eight times better than human eyes. This helps them spot prey hiding in grass or trees from high in the sky.

Some hawks chase birds through thick trees. Others sit and wait, then dive down fast. Each kind of hawk has its own special way to hunt.

FLYING SOUTH

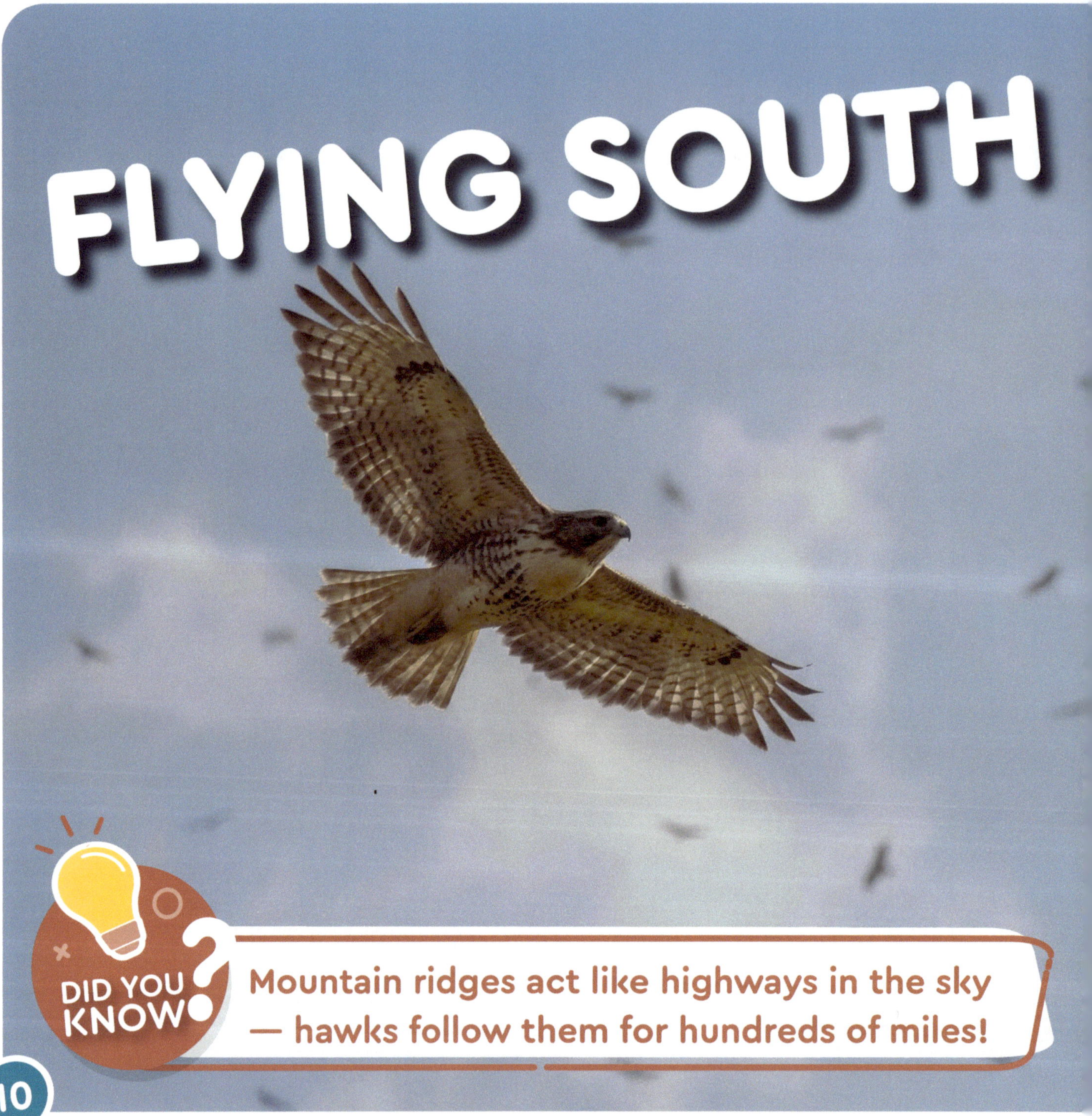

DID YOU KNOW?

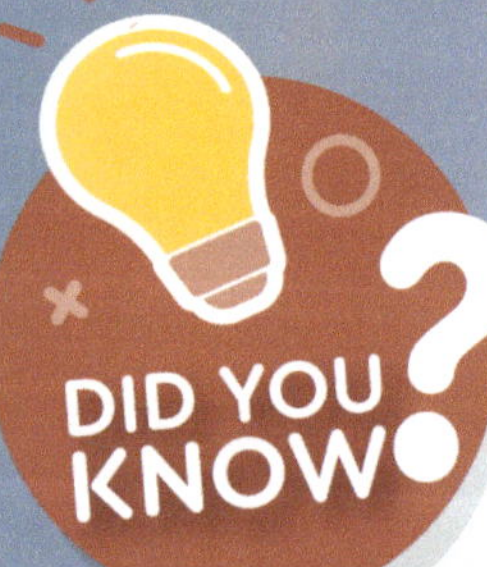

Mountain ridges act like highways in the sky — hawks follow them for hundreds of miles!

Whoosh! Hundreds of hawks stream across the autumn sky.

Each fall, many hawks fly south for winter. This long trip is called **migration**. To save energy, hawks ride bubbles of warm rising air called **thermals**.

Thermals form over the ground on sunny days. Hawks circle inside them and go up, up, up. Then they glide a long way before catching the next one. Some hawks travel hundreds of miles without flapping once!

Look at the sky in fall. You may see lines of hawks flying by. On a good day, thousands can pass by one spot in just a few hours!

REDTAIL RISING

The red-tailed hawk's scream is the sound used for eagles in movies — Hollywood loves that fierce cry!

Keeeer! A red-tailed hawk screams from its tree perch.

Red-tailed hawks are easy to spot. They often sit on poles and signs by the road. Their red-brown tail gives them their name, but only adults have it. Young red-tails have striped brown tails instead.

These hawks eat mice, rabbits, and snakes. They watch from high up, then swoop down to grab a meal. You can hear their loud cry from far away.

Red-tails live in forests, fields, and deserts. They build big stick nests in tall trees. Some pairs use the same nest year after year, adding more sticks each time.

URBAN ATTACKERS

Cooper's hawks can fly over 50 miles per hour — fast enough to catch a pigeon in midair!

DID YOU KNOW?

Zoom! A Cooper's hawk zips between the trees like a jet.

Cooper's hawks are at home in cities and towns. They have learned to hunt small birds near bird feeders and parks. Their short wings and long tail help them weave through tight spaces at top speed.

These hawks are about the size of a crow. They have blue-gray backs and rusty striped chests. Up close, their bright red eyes really stand out.

If a Cooper's hawk shows up in your yard, smaller birds hide fast. They know a predator is near! Songbirds will freeze or dive into bushes until the danger passes.

SPEEDY SHARPSHINS

Zip! A sharp-shinned hawk darts through the branches.

Sharp-shinned hawks are the smallest hawks in North America. They look a lot like a Cooper's hawk but are only about the size of a blue jay. Do not let their size fool you though, these tiny hawks are fast and fierce.

Sharpshins hunt small birds in the woods. They zip through the trees and strike with a burst of speed. Their long tail helps them make quick, sharp turns between branches.

Males are much smaller than females. A female sharpshin can be almost twice the size of a male! Scientists think this helps the pair hunt different sizes of prey.

PRAIRIE TITAN

Thwump! A big hawk lands on a fence post in the wide prairie.

The ferruginous hawk is the biggest hawk in North America. It can spread its wings over four feet wide. Its name means rusty because of the red-brown color on its legs and back.

These hawks live in open prairies and grasslands. They hunt ground squirrels, rabbits, and prairie dogs. Unlike most hawks, they often watch for prey from a low perch or even from the ground itself.

Ferruginous hawks need wide open land. When prairies are turned into farms, these hawks lose their homes. Keeping grasslands safe helps these giants survive.

PACK HUNTERS

Yelp, yelp! Two hawks dive at a rabbit from either side.

Harris's hawks are the only hawks that hunt in teams. A group of three to seven birds works together like a wolf pack. One hawk may scare prey out of a bush while others wait to grab it.

These dark brown hawks live in the desert Southwest. They perch on cactus tops and tall poles. Their long legs help them stand on prickly plants without getting hurt.

Harris's hawks share food and help raise each other's young. Family members stick together for years. They are the most social hawks in the world!

ARCTIC ARRIVAL

22

Brrrr! A rough-legged hawk hunts over the frozen tundra.

Rough-legged hawks come from the far north. They are one of only three American hawks with feathers all the way down to their toes. This keeps them warm in the bitter Arctic cold.

In summer, they nest on high cliffs near the Arctic Circle. They eat small animals like mice and voles. When winter comes, they fly south to open fields in the United States.

Rough-legged hawks have a special skill. They can hover in one spot in the air, flapping and holding still to look for prey on the ground below.

SHOULDER SHOUT

Kee-ah! A red-shouldered hawk shouts from the treetops.

Red-shouldered hawks are some of the loudest hawks around. Their call rings through the forest all day long. Blue jays even copy their call to scare other birds away from feeders!

These hawks live in wet woods near streams and ponds. They hunt frogs, lizards, and snakes in the shallow water. Look for the red patches on their wings to know who they are.

Red-shouldered hawks come back to the same woods each year. A pair may live in one forest for their whole life, raising chicks in the same tree.

FOREST FLIER

26

Swoop! A broad-winged hawk drops from a branch and snatches its lunch.

Broad-winged hawks are small but tough. They spend their summers deep in eastern forests, hunting from low branches where the trees grow thick. Frogs, mice, and big insects do not stand a chance!

Their short, wide wings are built for darting between trees. They can twist and turn through a dense forest without missing a beat.

When fall arrives, broad-wings make one of the longest journeys in the hawk world. They fly all the way to Central and South America — a trip of over 4,000 miles!

WORLD TRAVELER

Swainson's hawks sometimes follow tractors across fields to catch bugs stirred up by the machines!

Flap, flap, glide! A Swainson's hawk begins its long trip south.

Swainson's hawks make one of the longest trips of any hawk. Each fall, they fly from North America all the way to Argentina. That is more than 6,000 miles each way!

In summer, these hawks live in open grasslands and fields. They eat lots of bugs along with mice and gophers. Farmers love them because they gobble up pests that hurt crops.

Big flocks of Swainson's hawks travel together. The trip south takes about two months. They cross deserts, mountains, and many countries to reach their winter home on the grassy plains of South America.

GOSHAWK FURY

The name goshawk means goose hawk — these fierce birds are big enough to catch a goose!

Crash! A goshawk blasts through the trees after its prey.

The northern goshawk is the toughest hunter in the forest. It is big and strong with thick legs and fierce red eyes. This hawk zooms through the trees at top speed to catch prey.

Goshawks eat squirrels, rabbits, and other birds. They are fast and fearless. A goshawk will crash right through thick branches to catch its meal, even if it means getting scratched.

These hawks guard their nests like no other bird. They will swoop at anyone who comes too close — hikers, dogs, even bears! If you hear angry screaming in the woods, back away slowly.

VULTURE CAMO

DID YOU KNOW?
Zone-tailed hawks are master copycats — even their black feathers and banded tails match vultures!

Swoop! A zone-tailed hawk drops from a group of vultures.

The zone-tailed hawk has a sneaky trick. It looks and flies just like a turkey vulture. Animals do not run from vultures because vultures only eat dead things. No danger there, right? Wrong!

The zone-tailed hawk hides in plain sight. It soars with a group of vultures, rocking its wings the same way they do. Then it suddenly drops down and grabs a lizard or small bird.

This trick works because the prey never sees the hawk coming. It thinks every bird up there is a harmless vulture. Surprise!

HARRIER HEARING
DID YOU KNOW?
A northern harrier can hear a mouse squeak from over 100 feet away!
34

Shhhh! A northern harrier listens for mice in the grass.

Northern harriers hunt like no other hawk. They fly low over fields and marshes, listening for sounds. Their round face works like a dish to catch sounds, just like an owl's face does.

Harriers have long wings and tails. They tip and tilt as they glide just above the grass. A white patch above their tail makes them easy to spot from far away.

Male harriers are gray and females are brown. They nest on the ground in tall grass, hidden from view. The male brings food to the female and young until the chicks can fly.

FALCONRY FRIENDS

Hup! A hawk leaps from a falconer's glove and takes flight.

People have trained hawks to hunt for a very long time. This sport is called falconry. A falconer builds trust with a hawk over many weeks of patient work.

Harris's hawks are a top pick for falconry. They are calm and smart. They learn fast and like to work with people. A falconer wears a thick leather glove so the hawk can land safely on their hand.

The hawk is always free to fly away. It stays because the falconer has earned its trust. That special bond is what makes falconry so amazing.

HAWK WATCH

Hawk Mountain in Pennsylvania was the world's first refuge made to protect hawks — it opened in 1934!

Wheet! A hawk whistles as it glides past a group of hikers.

Hawk watching is a fun way to enjoy nature. In fall, people sit on hilltops to count hawks as they fly by. All you need are your eyes and some patience. Binoculars help too!

Hawks need our help to stay safe. Wild places give them room to nest and hunt. Keeping water clean and planting trees helps them too. Every bit of nature we protect helps hawks survive.

You can help hawks from home. Learn to spot them. Tell your friends what you know. The more people care about hawks, the safer these amazing birds of prey will be.

GLOSSARY

prey
An animal that is hunted and eaten by another animal

talons
The sharp, curved claws on a hawk's feet

migration
A long trip animals make to find food or warmer weather

thermals
Bubbles of warm air that rise up from the ground

raptor
A bird that hunts other animals for food